D1241119

ART NOUVEAU
THE STYLE OF THE 1890s

ART NOUVEAU
THE STYLE OF THE 1890s

General Editor
Francesco Abbate

Translated by
Elizabeth Evans

PEERAGE BOOKS

English edition first published by Octopus Books
This edition published by Peerage Books
59 Grosvenor Street
London W1

Translation © 1972 Octopus Books

Originally published in Italian by
Gruppo Editoriale Fabbri S.p.A.

© 1966 Gruppo Editoriale Fabbri S.p.A., Milan

ISBN 0 907408 14 1

Printed in Italy by Gruppo Editoriale Fabbri S.p.A.

CONTENTS

THE ART NOUVEAU PERIOD

The turn of the nineteenth century was a complex period of intense activities, so rich in innovations in every field that it must be regarded as one of the most decisive eras in the history of European civilization. For society was then changing in many fundamental ways as technical progress, the growth of industry and new economic factors created not just new problems, but also a new type of society. The aristocracy had lost much of its power and the bourgeoisie, after a period of great wealth and prosperity, was now threatened by moral and financial crises; in contrast the masses were growing increasingly self-aware, inspired by a new revolutionary mood. The turn of the century was marked by the first political disturbances, the first strikes, the first claims for human rights, all of which were inspired and inflamed by anarchical and socialist theories spreading rapidly through the countries of Europe. It was in this period of ferment and pressing demand for change, in an atmosphere of polemics, decadence and new ideals that some of the basic premises of modern art were first uttered.

The cultural scene shows a wide variety of conflicting reactions to these influences, which obviously reflect the very complexity of the situation. For this was a period of extraordinary contrasts embracing both the final glories of the Belle Epoque and the explosion of new social demands and pressures, a continuance of old traditions and the statement of new ideals, the intimity of Marcel Proust and the more popular theories behind Art Nouveau. And so, too, the most talented and interesting personalities of the age were continually in contact with a wide variety of fresh ideas and attitudes. In Paris, for example the circle of people connected with the *Revue Blanche* represented a new type of intellectual élite, holding left-wing and anarchical opinions yet – and here lay the paradox – they were highly sophisticated people, indeed their leader was one of the most fascinating and sought-after men in Paris. If this should not seem unusual today, it was certainly not the case in the 1890s.

Several of the great masters of Impressionism were still active at this period and around the turn of the century, their creative talent undiminished. Renoir, after a period spent renewing his acquaintance with classical traditions, was now living in southern France. There he devoted himself with redoubled vigour to painting bright open-air landscapes in which the light and heat of the sun are made to caress and enhance natural forms. Monet was dedicated to capturing the infinitely subtle variations in the appearance of things produced by shifts of atmosphere and the changing times of day. He had gradually limited the range of his optical experiments while at

1   *Paul Sérusier (1863–1927) : Meditation. c 1890. Private Collection, Paris.*

1   Paul Sérusier (1863–1927): *Meditation. c* 1890. Private Collection, Paris. Photograph courtesy of the Foto Archivio, Galleria del Levante, Milan.
Sérusier's meeting with Gauguin at Pont-Aven in 1888 had a decisive influence on his painting which became more rhythmical and expressive.

2   Paul Sérusier (1863–1927): *The shower. c* 1895. Mlle Henriette Boutaric Collection, Paris.
The Nabis or 'prophets' were a group of painters formed by Sérusier whose main influence was Gauguin; among themselves they used nicknames and Sérusier was known as the prophet of the shining beard.

3   Maurice Denis (1870–1943): *The red roofs. c* 1892. Private Collection, Saint-Germain-en-Laye.
Denis, the theorist of the Nabis, wrote: 'Remember that a picture . . . is essentially a flat surface covered with colours assembled in a certain order'.

4   Maurice Denis (1870–1943): *The muses* (detail). 1893. Musée National d'Art Moderne, Paris.
Denis' affinity with the Nabis is obvious in this canvas, in which forms and colours swirl and blend together.

5   Paul-Elie Ranson (1862–1909): *The snake charmer c* 1890. Private Collection, Stockholm. Photograph courtesy of the Foto Archivio, Galleria del Levante, Milan.
Ranson was the only Nabi to abandon the easel and concentrate on tapestries based on traditional folk legends.

6   Ker-Xavier Roussel (1867–1944): *The wood-nymph.* Private Collection, Paris.
Apart from the subject-matter there is little resemblance to classical legend; the figure and the surrounding landscape shimmer with symbolic uncertainty.

2   *Paul Sérusier (1863–1927) : The shower. c 1895.*
Mlle Henriette Boutaric Collection, Paris.

3 *Maurice Denis (1870–1943) : The red roofs. c 1892. Private Collection,*
Saint-Germain-en-Laye.

4 *Maurice Denis (1870–1943) : The muses. 1893. Musée National d'Art Moderne, Paris.*

5   *Paul-Elie Ranson (1862–1909) : The snake charmer.
c 1890. Private Collection, Stockholm.*

6　*Ker-Xavier Roussel (1867–1944) : The wood-nymph. Private Collection, Paris.*

work on the impressive Rouen Cathedral series, which expressed his growing desire to separate elements of stable forms into overall harmonies of subtle colour; this tendency was to find its full expression in his later water-lily series. Dégas was now old and almost blind, but was still painting his female nudes and dancers. Carnille Pissarro had abandoned his experiments in Divisionism and returned to the natural freshness of the Impressionist landscape. And so it was that the lyrical naturalism inspired by a rediscovery of the open-air, which had been such a revolutionary innovation in the second half of the nineteenth century, was still clearly an active force at the turn of the century. It appeared in other forms in Germany, with characteristic touches of late-Romanticism, and its leading exponents were the so-called German Impressionists led by Max Liebermann and including Corinth and Slevogt, whose violent colours and line show that they were also part of a completely new movement.

Naturalism also gave rise to other artistic movements inspired by the idea of applying their principles in intellectual, rather scientific ways. The Divisionists claimed to see a basic order in reality, which they studied and painted according to certain optical laws, supporting their case by evidence taken from the studies of contemporary scientists. So too Cézanne went beyond Impressionism in his passionate efforts to organize nature, establishing the basis for a method of visual abstraction by which the reality the eye first observes is interpreted and given an order by the use of the intellect. Elsewhere there were artists who reacted – as Cézanne himself did – against the Impressionists' contemplative attitude to reality, but

18

7 Ker-Xavier Roussel (1867–1944) : Milking the goat. 1891.
Salomon Collection, Paris.

7   Ker-Xavier Roussel (1867–1944): *Milking the goat.* 1891. Salomon Collection, Paris.
These expressive, gently distorted figures show the artist stretching his material in the search for a new and vigorous idiom.

8   Pierre Bonnard (1867–1947): *The checkered blouse.* 1892. Musée National d'Art Moderne, Charles Terrasse Collection, Paris.
It was only at the outset of his career that Bonnard was affected by the concern for order of the other Nabis; he generally preferred painting zones of colour and the patterns of clothes and materials just as the eye saw them rather than in a formal sequence.

9   Pierre Bonnard (1867–1947): Poster for *La Revue Blanche.* 1894. Bibliothèque Nationale, Paris.
Bonnard designed several posters for *La Revue Blanche*, the avant-garde Parisian periodical founded by the Natanson brothers in 1891. He also did ironical and sophisticated illustrations for the magazine itself.

10   Pierre Bonnard (1867–1947): *Montmartre. c* 1900. Phillips Collection, Washington, DC.
Pierre Bonnard was closely associated with the Symbolist movement and his careful study of Japanese prints led him also to insert something of their luminosity in his paintings.

11   Pierre Bonnard (1867–1947): *Lunch beneath the lamplight.* 1898. Private Collection, Montreux.
This simple domestic scene shows that Bonnard's portrayal of intimate moments consisted not so much of a study of reality as the creation of an atmosphere where time past is called with an almost Proustian intensity.

8   *Pierre Bonnard (1867–1947) : The checkered blouse. 1892. Musée National d'Art Moderne, Paris.*

Bonnard
1892

9   *Pierre Bonnard (1867–1947) : Poster for La Revue Blanche.*
1894. Bibliothèque Nationale, Paris.

10   *Pierre Bonnard (1867–1947) : Montmartre. c 1900. Phillips Collection, Washington, DC.*

11   *Pierre Bonnard (1867–1947) : Lunch beneath the lamplight. 1898. Private Collection, Montreux.*

then turned their attention to the problems of representing chance situations in a fleeting world. This sponsored a new interest in social criticism and the examination of character – both of which were important features in the diffuse pattern of artistic thinking at the turn of the century. Toulouse-Lautrec was perhaps the most authoritative of the new 'voices', but other, lesser artists such as Carrière should be considered in this context, also illustrators such as Steinlen and Raffaëlli, and a younger generation of artists among whom were Jacques Villon and Georges Rouault. Even Bonnard and other members of the Nabis such as Vallotton and Maurice Denis show examples of penetrating social criticism, though in an intimate key and pervaded by a subtle vein of decadence.

Other artists occupied less extreme positions, one of which might be described as a blend of romantic naturalism – inspired by the Impressionists – and a more restless outlook more in keeping with an age that actively pursued new forms of expression. In this broad category belong the leading contemporary sculptors, Rosso in Italy and Rodin in France, as well as Antoine Bourdelle in his early work. They obviously understood the instability of their situation, in which old ideals were no longer valid and a radical evolution in all fields of art was clearly under way.

There was also a current of escapism running through the art of those years encouraged no doubt by the prevailing mood of restlessness and insecurity, and doubt about established values. It was expressed in a taste for the exotic, and a new interest in primitive people (Gauguin's experiences were here of decisive importance). The primitivism of the naive painters was another aspect of this same escapism; the ingenuous Rousseau helped others to rediscover life's pure inherent poetry, which he expressed directly, stripped of all its inessential trappings. Symbolism, too, was a product of the desire to extend experience, and its influence in all fields of European art was enormous. It affected French artists from Moreau to Redon, Gauguin to Sérusier; in Belgium and Germany it was taken up by men like Toorop, Max Klinger, Hodler and Klimt. It was also expressed in the literature, drama and music of the time. Symbolism was born from a desire to penetrate beyond the formal appearance of reality, and to use art to express the profound and mysterious values that lay behind the veiled essence of things. It is hardly surprising that Symbolism should have been so influential at such a time of spiritual crisis; it spread to many forms of art and shared a current of morbid and yet refined decadence with the works of Art Nouveau.

At the same time Art Nouveau was also inspired by revolutionary theories that were very firmly based in reality. These resolutely original and forward-looking ideas had previously been expressed in the mid-nineteenth century by the Arts and Crafts Movement and by the Pre-Raphaelites. They were the theories of 'useful art', an art that would appeal to the masses because it was applied to daily life and because it was practical and educational. The concept of applied art was firmly upheld at this time when industry was supplanting craftsmanship and architectural theories were changing radically, with a new emphasis on the functional rather than the purely aesthetic.

The first exponent of these ideas was the Englishman William Morris, whose influence is clear in the work

12   *Edouard Vuillard (1868–1940) : The newspaper.*
Phillips Collection, Washington, DC.

12　Edouard Vuillard (1868–1940): *The newspaper*. Phillips Collection, Washington, DC.

Vuillard came from a middle-class background and enjoyed painting scenes of family life set in modest but luminous interiors, animated by the artist's affection for his subject.

13　Edouard Vuillard (1868–1940): *The pebble beach*. Salomon Collection, Paris.

Vuillard's compositions have rhythm and elegance and his low-keyed tones are varied with an occasional vivid contrast.

14　Edouard Vuillard (1868–1940): *Lady in blue*. 1890. Salomon Collection, Paris.

This painting records with great attention to detail the room in Ranson's house where the Nabis used to meet. In their half-joking, half-mystical way they called it 'le temple'.

15　Edouard Vuillard (1868–1940): *Married life*. 1900. Private Collection, Paris.

This domestic scene shows a couple caught in silence together. The style is edgier and more nervous than the previous example, and the sober colours echo the grave atmosphere in the room.

13   *Edouard Vuillard (1868–1940) : The pebble beach. Salomon
Collection, Paris.*

14   *Edouard Vuillard (1868–1940)* : *Lady in blue.* *1890.* Salomon
Collection, Paris.

15 *Edouard Vuillard (1868–1940) : Married life. 1900. Private Collection, Paris.*

of the Belgians Van de Velde, Horta and Berlage, in France in that of Guimard, Perret, Gallé and Majorelle, and in Scotland that of Mackintosh. All the figurative arts underwent the same influence and the Nabis designed posters and illustrations in accordance with the theory that applied art should be made available to the masses. In much the same spirit Klimt decorated the Palais Stoclet with mosaics and other artists produced designs for furniture, china, textiles and stained glass. Yet others used their vivid imaginations to criticize society in a more direct fashion, altering the appearance of reality by means of distortion. Their style contains grotesque and visionary elements, such as the mad masks of James Ensor and Edward Munch's hallucinatory images. By working within a traditional framework, to which they brought the new and dramatic language of Expressionism, these artists opened an important avenue of development for art in the decades to come; certainly theirs was a major addition to the complex pattern of influences that has inspired so much of twentieth century art.

Gauguin had the greatest impact on the style and theories of a group of artists who called themselves the Nabis after the Hebrew word for prophet. Their work has much in common with Symbolism – and their choice of name indicates the essentially idealistic direction of their aims. They dreamed of creating a purified art, rich in moral content and representing lofty spiritual concepts in a Symbolist manner. It was Paul Sérusier, the theorist of the group, who together with Maurice Denis spread the message of Gauguin, whom Sérusier met in Pont-Aven, among their friends at the Académie Julien (who included

Ranson, Ibels, Roussel, Bonnard and Vuillard and others such as Lacombe and the Swiss Vallotton).

Maurice Denis describes the following events: 'It was when we came back from Pont-Aven in 1888 that the name of Gauguin was revealed to us in a rather mysterious way by Sérusier. He showed us the lid of a cigar box on which a landscape was painted so sketchily that it was almost indistinguishable in violet, vermilion, green and other pure colours almost straight as they came from the tube, without any addition of white. . . . Once, in the Bois d'Amour Gauguin had said, "How do you see that tree? It is green? Well, paint it with the richest green on your palette. Is that shadow blue? Make it pure ultramarine. . . ."'

The Nabis established a brotherhood with complicated rites and their meetings took place in Ranson's *atelier* – known by the mystic name 'le temple'. Although they made an important contribution to the culture of the time and were an interesting phenomenon during those difficult transitional years following the zenith of Impressionism, the Nabis are really famous for the fact that in their early days Bonnard and Vuillard, both outstanding personalities, were associated with the group. As a group the Nabis stayed together only a few years. Although they remained friends the artists soon went their own ways: Denis, Sérusier and the Dutchman Jean Verkade (who was shortly to take religious orders) were drawn together by their mutual interest in a spiritual and mystic vision, and this tended to isolate them from the less religious members of the group; while Vallotton, Vuillard and Bonnard were in time to rank among the greatest of modern artists.

17 *Félix Vallotton (1865–1925) : Woman searching in a cupboard. 1900.*
Willi Raeber Collection, Basle.

16 *Félix Vallotton (1865–1925) : Women with cats. Galerie Vallotton, Lausanne.*

37

16   Félix Vallotton (1865–1925): *Women with cats*. 1898. Galerie Vallotton, Lausanne.

A talented and original artist, Félix Vallotton painted realistic interiors with a satirical, rather bitter tone that often suggests a deep inner tension.

17   Félix Vallotton (1865–1925): *Woman searching in a cupboard*.1900. Willi Raeber Collection, Basle.

The superficial coldness of some of Vallotton's canvases arises partly through his willingness to experiment with techniques of composition.

18   Félix Vallotton (1865–1925): *At the café*. 1909. H. Hahnloser Collection, Berne.

In this rather cynical work the bland, insensitive features of the men are contrasted with a sharp white triangle representing feminine rapacity and shrewishness; the woman's hat with its huge, ostentatious feather, is also used to make a social comment.

19   Félix Vallotton (1865–1925): *A street in the old quarter of Marseilles*. Richard Buchler Collection, Winterthur.

Vallotton painted scenes from daily life reminiscent of Bonnard and Vuillard, although his compositions are more precise and more static, as if Vallotton wanted to fix for ever the reality he observed.

20   Félix Vallotton (1865–1925): *The estuary at Honfleur*. 1911. Galerie Vallotton, Lausanne.

The development of Vallotton's style is most apparent in his later landscapes, which are conveyed in bold outlines and give an impression of emptiness and unreality.

18 *Félix Vallotton (1865–1925)* : *At the café.* **1909**. *H. Hahnloser Collection, Berne.*

19 *Félix Vallotton (1865–1925) : A street in the old quarter of Marseilles.*
Richard Buchler Collection, Winterthur.

20   *Félix Vallotton (1865–1925) : The estuary at Honfleur. 1911. Galerie
Vallotton, Lausanne.*

It was the reality of the daily round, the close intimacy of domestic interiors, with their familiar objects and figures, that inspired the work of Vuillard. He lovingly reveals all the small details of his personal world: flat areas of colours are enclosed within elegant linear arabesques vibrating with a sentimental intensity that is the great fascination of Vuillard's work. This same emotional intensity and humble, even melancholic devotion to the secret truths of a modest existence are also characteristic of Bonnard's art. Bonnard turned to his own experience and the inmost recesses of his memory to find images that best recalled the lost world of time past, whose emotions and sensations live on. He painted this tenderly passionate and magical world of daily life in vibrant, low-keyed tones. His scenes of affectionate recollection, sometimes marked by a note of gentle and attractive irony, are bathed in an atmosphere of sentimental enjoyment and sweet nostalgia.

Besides the Nabis other artists in Europe at the turn of the century were influenced by these various elements of Symbolism and the idea of using an intensely personal approach. The Danish artist Willumsen followed the lead of Gauguin and Redon, while in Belgium Evenepoel and in England Sickert adopted a more intimate manner in their works that held vague echoes of Bonnard. The Norwegian Edvard Munch was linked with the Nabis; he was an artist of extraordinary expressive power and obsessed with inner problems. A friend of Ibsen and Strindberg, he was the spiritual heir to the deep anguish, the obsession with the problems of life and death that are characteristic of the Norwegian race, with their wealth of legends and atavistic fears. Munch's art combines this dark and primordial Nordic strain with the decorative Symbolism of the French school and the result is richly expressive. His style is both violent and disciplined and perfectly expresses his complex subjects. His figures are delineated with curving, sinuous contours against a fluid, unearthly void, taking on the ephemeral and disturbing appearance of phantoms. Munch's palette is harsh and cold and he sometimes combined unusual colours to produce arresting and even jarring effects, thereby accentuating the nature and message of the painting, as for example in the famous *Scream* (see illustration 30). Munch's work was greatly admired in Paris, but he was a highly controversial figure both in Norway and in Germany, where he lived from 1892–1908. When he returned to Norway he modified his style with lighter colours and less severe forms. Although Munch produces some remarkable works in this later period he is chiefly known for the great vigour of his early canvases, by virtue of which he is considered the most important early exponent of Expressionism.

The work of the Belgian James Ensor is certainly on a level with that of Munch. He was a founder member (1884) of the Société des XX (Twenty), a group of painters born in Belgium that included many of the most talented artists in the Low Countries. Ensor was inspired by the same visionary imagination as Munch. Symbolist tendencies, dating from his stay in France, combined with his own taste for strange hallucinatory effects and the grotesque or spectacular distortion of reality that is characteristic of early painting in the Low Countries, from Bosch to Brueghel. However, Ensor's painting was no cold imitation of traditional themes studied from early masters. His disturbing

21　*Walter Richard Sickert (1860–1942) :*
Aubrey Beardsley. 1894. Tate Gallery, London.

21   Walter Richard Sickert (1860–1942): *Aubrey Beardsley*. 1894. Tate Gallery, London.
This is a portrait of Aubrey Beardsley, the illustrator and editor of *The Yellow Book*, to which Sickert also contributed in 1894–5.

22   Henry Evenepoel (1872–99): *The Spaniard in Paris*. Musée des Beaux-Arts, Ghent.
Evenepoel painted some outstanding portraits and scenes of African life (he spent some time in Algeria); his work, painted at the end of the century, was an original combination of 'intimiste' suggestiveness, inspired by Bonnard, and Nabi symbolism.

23   James Ensor (1860–1949): *Skeletons trying to warm themselves* (detail). 1889. Private Collection, Fort Worth, Texas.
The artist is trying to suggest here not so much the levelling power of death as the desperate absurdity of the skeletons trying to regain life from the stove.

24   James Ensor (1860–1949): *Skeletons fighting over a smoked herring*. 1891. B. Goldschmidt Collection, Brussels.
This may represent two critics arguing about Ensor's work. He had begun his career painting in an Impressionist style and then during the 1880s changed to portraying fantastic and macabre scenes in a style that greatly influenced the Expressionist school.

25   James Ensor (1860–1949): *The rue de Flandre*. 1891. Musée Royal des Beaux-Arts, Antwerp.
The theme of streets decorated with bunting was a popular one and was painted by Manet and Monet in 1878, by van Gogh in 1886, by Dufy and Marquet in 1906 and again by Léger in 1914.

22   *Henry Evenepoel (1872–99) : The Spaniard in Paris. Musée des Beaux-Arts, Ghent.*

23 *James Ensor (1860–1949) : Skeletons trying to warm themselves
(detail). 1889. Private Collection, Fort Worth, Texas.*

24   *James Ensor (1860–1949) : Skeletons fighting over a smoked herring.*
1891. B. Goldschmidt Collection, Brussels.

25 *James Ensor (1860–1949) : The rue de Flandre. 1891. Musée Royal des Beaux-Arts, Brussels.*

visions of skeletons and other grotesque forms express moral and social protest with great violence and are, too, the creation of a genuinely original artist. All the same, he does not always manage to maintain the same extraordinary level of polemic vigour expressed in his most brilliant images; that there were limits to his vision can be seen in certain canvases that scarcely rise above the level of the bizarre anecdote.

The main trends in Belgian painting at the turn of the century are revealed in the work of the Société des XX. Their principal roots were in French cultural movements – Seurat's Divisionism and the Symbolism of the Nabis group – but between them they reflected all the intellectual trends in European art of the time. Artists had a tendency to concentrate increasingly on exquisite decorative motifs, and harmonious curvilinear patterns shown against flat zones of colour. However, it was never a purely ornamental style, its formal preciosity hid symbolic allusions and in every aspect of a painting the artist's inner feelings are apparent, in line, form and colour. This applies to the work of Fernand Khnopff, whose powerful sensibility is apparent in the graphic elegance of his compositions; and to Jan Toorop, who initially used a Divisionist technique, but then changed his style radically after meeting Redon and the English graphic artist Beardsley. He then became less interested in colour and concentrated on evolving a style based on the rhythmic and sinuous possibilities of line, one that was also rich in evocative symbols.

Henry van de Velde also belonged initially to this movement. He was an extraordinary artist with interests in every field from painting and architecture to all forms of applied art. He became associated with the leading *fin-de-siècle* movements in a number of countries, where they flourished as either Art Nouveau, or Stile Liberty or Jugendstil or Sezessionstil or Modern Style.

Although Art Nouveau is concerned with ornament and embraces decadence, it also constitutes a real attempt to define the social function of art, and as such it was chiefly influential in the fields of architecture and the applied arts. Even so, painting was also affected, and van de Velde himself, whose early works are clearly Divisionist like those of all the leading artists of the Société des XX, later inspired all contemporary art by his highly refined designs for furniture and house interiors.

The fascination for line and its ornamental value gave a new importance to graphic art and attracted specialists to this field, and many graphic works of great aesthetic value were produced. Beardsley waä undoubtedly the best of the graphic artists, but the talented French artists Jules Chéret and Eugène Grasset also designed lively posters and lithographs.

The two great centres of German painting were in Munich and Berlin. At the end of the nineteenth century many conflicting trends influenced German artists, ranging from the work of the still active late Romantics and a fairly conventional sort of Impressionism imported from France to an increasingly important current of Symbolism encouraged by the work of the Norwegian Munch, who was at that time living in Berlin. Max Klinger, in numerous paintings, and von Stuck were the first to express general dissatisfaction with the work of the rather mediocre and traditional German artists of the day.

Max Liebermann was then the chief exponent of

26   *Edvard Munch (1863–1944) : The sick girl. 1885–6. Nasjonalgalleriet, Oslo.*

27   *Edvard Munch
(1863–1944) :
Spring day in the
Karl-Johanstrasse.
1891. Munch
Museet, Oslo.*

26   Edvard Munch (1863–1944): *The sick girl.* 1885–6. Nasjonalgalleriet, Oslo.

This tenderly observed scene is also highly charged with emotive elements, apparent in the choice of colours as well as in the composition of the figures.

27   Edvard Munch (1863–1944): *Spring day in the Karl-Johanstrasse.* 1891. Munch Meseet, Oslo.

This painting shows how Munch attempted at one time to use Impressionist techniques – even though his talents, especially his great flair for psychological interpretation, were not suited to the optical realism of the Impressionists.

28   Edvard Munch (1863–1944): *The storm.* 1893. Christian Mustad Collection, Oslo.

Munch explored an interior landscape with great intensity, producing an individual language of symbolism and sensual expressionism. He had an especially important influence on German and Scandinavian painting and became closely involved with artistic circles in Berlin from 1892–1908.

29   Edvard Munch (1863–1944): *Summer night at Oslofjord. c* 1900. Städtische Kunsthalle, Mannheim.

The image of an island reflected in the dark sea looks like the elastic outline of a huge half-open mouth; the subject is here less important than the deep symbolic allusions.

30   Edvard Munch (1863–1944): *The scream.* 1893. Nasjonalgalleriet, Oslo.

'I heard this great scream coming from the whole of nature' – these words explain how in his painting Munch made landscape and nature seem to act in harmony with man's state of mind. This painting is now regarded as a key work in the history of Expressionism.

28 *Edvard Munch (1863–1944) : The storm. 1893. Christian Mustad Collection, Oslo.*

29 *Edvard Munch (1863–1944) : Summer night at Oslofjord. c 1900. Städtische Kunsthalle, Mannheim.*

German Impressionist painting, which as a movement had no great merit. His own work rarely went beyond conventional and superficial scenes recording domestic life and busy streets. Although he was obviously influenced by Millet his canvases have none of that artist's sincere humanitarianism, nor the spontaneous freshness of Impressionist painting. Corinth and Slevogt were more accurate and down-to-earth in their observations of the harsh Northern countryside. Younger than Liebermann, they were initially his admirers but later, after they had visited more sophisticated centres including Munich and Paris, their work outgrew Liebermann's conventional manner. The influences of Millet, the Barbizon school and French naturalism entered the work of these artists, especially that of Slevogt, who was the more imaginative and inclined in typical German fashion to interpret nature via a highly subjective process. The rich intensity of his palette and his excellent compositions show that he also had some regard for the growing current of Expressionism – which was also to affect Corinth.

Two of the most notable artists of the German school working at the turn of the century were influenced by the international school of Symbolism: the Swiss Ferdinand Hodler and the Austrian Gustav Klimt. After studying at the École des Beaux Arts in Geneva, Hodler's first canvases show good, careful draughtsmanship and technique; as yet, however, the artist is clearly undecided whether to follow the German tradition or the example of Corot. Very soon, though, the growing influence of Symbolism led him to express complex spiritual notions in stylized forms combining a plastic and linear approach. The result was fairly

30 *Edvard Munch (1863–1944): The scream. 1893.*
Nasjonalgalleriet, Oslo.

lifeless, even pompous, as his inspiration came from purely academic sources. His compositions were based on a contrast between stiff, rectilinear figures placed against a landscape that was reduced to its barest essentials and expressed in flat areas of colour applied with horizontal brushstrokes. Although he is considered an important figure in Central European painting Hodler's earlier work has little real artistic merit, for his excessive concentration on theory limited the spontaneity of his painting. The landscapes he produced at a much later period in the twentieth century are infinitely more successful because they depend far less on Symbolist theories. His style was more vigorous and successful when he was inspired by the severe beauty of Alpine landscapes.

Gustav Klimt interpreted Symbolism in a quite different way. His early painting is completely traditional, but his style began to evolve after he came under the influence of Beardsley, Toorop, Mackintosh and, more generally, the Art Nouveau movement. Decadence is the hallmark of Klimt's work, its exquisitely languid and refined linear patterns expressing all the anxiety and strife of passion and death so dear to contemporary poetry and literature. His paintings combine dazzling colours and an obsessional re-iteration of complex arabesques and ornamental motifs that evoke a sense of oriental extravagance as well as feelings of neurosis and deep disquiet. Between the rhythmic patterns of his lines appear visions of unexpectedly decadent human faces, wraeked by the violence of their passions and contrasting vividly with the intricate decorations surrounding them. The artist stresses this contrast by using little bits of silver and gold, which he applied between the rich orna-

31   *Johannes Theodoor Toorop (1858–1928) : Motherhood. Rijksmuseum Kröller-Müller, Otterlo.*

32 *Johannes Theodoor Toorop (1858–1928) : The three brides. 1893.*
Rijksmuseum Kröller-Müller, Otterlo.

65

31   Johannes Theodoor Toorop (1858–1928): *Mother-hood*. 1891. Rijksmuseum Kröller-Müller, Otterlo.
During his career Toorop worked in various styles including Impressionism and Divisionism; after his conversion to the Roman Catholic faith his art reflected his new beliefs.

32   Johannes Theodoor Toorop (1858–1928): *The three brides*. 1893. Rijksmuseum Kröller-Müller, Otterlo.
Toorop's later style had a great influence on the Art Nouveau movement, placing great emphasis on flat patterns of sensual curves and redolent with Decadent imagery. Here he deals with three stages of womanhood – the virgin bride, the wife and the *femme fatale*.

33   Johan Thorn Prikker (1868–1932): *The bride*. 1893. Rijksmuseum Kröller-Müller, Otterlo.
This painting shows a Christ figure and his bride surrounded by a menacing cluster of phallic tulips.

34   Franz von Stuck (1863–1928): *War*. Bayerische Staatsgemäldesammlungen, Munich.
Franz von Stuck, one of the founders of the Munich Secession, shared the obsessions of his fellow-German exhibitors for images of evil, death, the faun and the siren, which he painted with rhythmic lines and bold colour.

34   *Franz von Stuck (1863–1928) : War. Bayerische Staatsgemäldesammlungen, Munich.*

mental motifs and the powerfully expressive faces. Klimt had a great influence on Austrian painting and was the life and moving spirit of an artistic revival (in 1897 he founded the Vienna Secession) that was to embrace artists like Egon Schiele and Oskar Kokoschka.

In Italy Lombardy was among the most important artistic centres of the second half of the nineteenth century. It was there that the Scapigliatura movement flourished at about the time Impressionism was at its height. Started by a talented generation of restless young romantics, Scapigliatura affected both literature and the fine arts. Painters concentrated on studying the effects of light and the artist Daniele Ranzoni wrote: 'The line does not exist in nature or in art; only the effects of light are important'. Thus Tranquillo Cremona bathed his charming paintings in soft light, giving them an almost decadent suavity, and the sculptor Giuseppe Grandi suggested the volume and shape of his figures by concentrations of vibrant light on the rough, unfinished-looking surfaces of his work. This same apparent lack of finish, which nevertheless fully suggests the total composition, is characteristic of the paintings of Ranzoni. The people, and more rarely the landscapes that he paints with such charm and imagination are tentatively suggested in a few lightly sketched lines. The work of Medardo Rosso, the sculptor, is also typical of this cultural movement, hovering between a genuinely revolutionary form of modern art and adherence to past traditions.

Once Divisionism was initiated by Seurat it spread through Europe; in due time it reached Italy, where a highly talented artist called Giovanni Segantini became the leader of the new movement. He learnt of

35   *Lovis Corinth (1858–1925) : Sleeping nude (detail). Kunsthalle, Bremen.*

35　Lovis Corinth (1858–1925): *Sleeping nude* (detail). Kunsthalle, Bremen.
Corinth used a bold form of naturalism rather than a pure Impressionist technique which gave his work a feeling of spontaneity and warmth.

36　Max Slevogt (1868–1932): *The singer d'Andrade*. 1902. Niedersächsisches Landesmuseum, Hanover.
Slevogt began by using a dark palette typical of the sombre and dramatic style of northern painting, but subsequently worked more freely.

37　Gustav Klimt (1862–1918): *Salome* (detail). 1909. Galleria Internazionale d'Arte Moderna, Venice.
In this extraordinary painting a modern beauty is ensnared with her neuroses in a Kaleidoscope setting of Byzantine splendour.

38　Gustav Klimt (1862–1918): *The kiss*. Österreichische Galerie, Vienna.
The artist has carved out his two figures against a gold background; their robes contrast dramatically with the softly rendered facial features.

39　Gustav Klimt (1862–1918): *Schloss Kammer on the Attersee*. 1911. Österreichische Galerie, Vienna.
In this sparkling canvas Klimt has adopted a Divisionist technique, brining to it his great flair for intensive and dramatic colour.

40　Ferdinand Hodler (1853–1918): *Landscape near Caux with drifting clouds*. 1917. Kunsthaus, Zurich.
In comparison with the totally anti-naturalistic paintings of his Symbolist phase Ferdinand Hodler seems more receptive to nature in this later period and more sensitive to colour and light.

36   Max Slevogt *(1868–1932)* : *The singer d'Andrade. 1902.*
Niedersächsisches Landesmuseum, Hanover.

37 *Gustav*
Klimt (1862–
1918) : Salome
(detail). 1909.
Galleria Inter-
Internazionale
d'Arte
Moderna,
Venice.

38   *Gustav Klimt (1862–1918) : The kiss. Österreichische Galerie, Vienna.*

39   *Gustav Klimt
(1862–1918):
Schloss Kammer on
the Attersee. 1911.
Österreichische
Galerie, Vienna.*

40   *Ferdinand Hodler (1853–1918) : Landscape near Caux with drifting
clouds. 1917. Kunsthaus, Zurich.*

Seurat's ideas through another of Divisionism's great exponents, Grubicy, and then applied them in his own original way to evolve a style that is a harmonious combination of naturalistic observation and symbolic allusion. These paintings show his truly poetic inspiration and real love of nature – the deep emotional response he made to silent mountain landscapes. However, at a later period his lyrical tendency waä spoiled by too much emphasis on mystical symbolism. In fact when he went to live in the Engadine in Switzerland he gave an increasingly literary emphasic to his work and this ultimately detracted from the freshness of his style. Similarly the work of Gaetano Previati is limited by an academic and conventional symbolism, although his illustrations have a certain spontaneous charm; he saw Divisionism as a technique and concentrated on perfecting it, rather at the expense of his own personal poetic vision. This is also true in some respects of Morbelli and Pellizza da Volpedo, who sought also to expound social theories through their work. Pellizza da Volpedo was in fact an artist of great creative talent, but those of his paintings that express a political or social view are less successful than his anecdotal scenes of humble daily existence.

The tradition of landscape painting flourished until the end of the century in Lombardy and Piedmont, following the fine example set by the work of Fontanesi. The Lombard artist Emilio Gola bathed his scenes in a subtle atmosphere of nostalgia well suited to the countryside he painted, while Cesare Tallone composed imposing mountain scenes that have an outstanding three-dimensional quality.

In Piedmont Vittorio Avondo and Lorenzo Delleani

41   *Tranquillo Cremona (1837–78) : Maternal love. Civica Galleria d'Arte Moderna, Milan.*

41   Tranquillo   Cremona   (1837–78):   *Maternal   love.*
Civica Galleria d'Arte Moderna, Milan.
Tranquillo Cremona was one of the leading artists of the
Scapigliatura movement in Lombardy. He often used
effects of light to make his subdued forms glow against
their subtle backgrounds.

42   Tranquillo Cremona (1837–78): *Listening* (detail).
Private Collection, Turin.
Having studied the great masters of the fifteenth and
sixteenth centuries in Venice Cremona became exclusively a figure painter; he is best known for his graceful
if sentimental portraits of women.

43   Daniele Ranzoni (1843–89): *View of Lake Maggiore.*
Civica Galleria d'Arte Moderna, Milan; Grassi Collection.
While in his portraits he often reshaped the appearance
of reality to suggest character and inner meanings,
Ranzoni's landscapes show a more direct and spontaneous
naturalism.

44   Ernesto Bazzano (1859–1937): *Self-portrait.* Civica
Galleria d'Arte Moderna, Milan.
At the outset of his career Ernesto Bazzano was a faithful
follower of Grandi and naturalism, but later his style was
inspired by a desire to bring out the light-reflecting
values of his surfaces.

45   Giuseppe Grandi (1843–94): *Study.* Civica Galleria
d'Arte Moderna, Milan.
Grandi built up this work by adding on finely modelled
pieces of clay until the light-reflecting surfaces were
animated to his satisfaction.

43 Daniele Ranzoni (1843–89) : *View of Lake Maggiore. Civica Galleria d'Arte Moderna, Milan.*

44 *Ernesto Bazzano (1859–1937) : Self-portrait.*
Civica Galleria d'Arte Moderna, Milan.

45   *Giuseppe Grandi (1843–94) : Study. Civica Galleria d'Arte
Moderna, Milan.*

continued the naturalist tradition, which in the work of Enrico Reycend came close to an Impressionist style with its freshness and spontaneity. The tradition of realistic sketches depicting humble scenes was carried on by the Roman Antonio Mancini, whose style was charming but only superficially effective; and by the Venetian Giacomo Favretto, who attempted in his narrative scenes to follow the eighteenth century tradition of Longhi's *genre* painting. Also from Venice Ciardi, a painter influenced by Macchiaioli, produced a number of landscapes (though these are of no great merit).

Those artists who managed to travel and come into direct contact with the various European cultural movements were more successful: Federico Zandomeneghi, Giovanni Boldini and Giuseppe de Nittis are obvious examples. Zandomeneghi went to Paris in 1874 and met various Impressionists; under their influence he evolved an intimate and suggestive style full of all the vibrant atmosphere of Impressionist painting as well as a certain Venetian warmth. The work of Giovanni Boldini, who became a fashionable society painter in France, occasionally surprises the observer by his vivacity and keen observation in portraits and scenes of busy Paris streets. These in fact provide a brilliant record of Parisian life in the Belle Époque. Giuseppe de Nittis' views – famous throughout Europe – of Paris and London are more refined and deal in delicate chromatic effects.

It took longer for European sculpture to accept and adopt the new ways of seeing things. Sculptors were more firmly rooted in tradition, and in fact the second half of the nineteenth century offers few interesting examples in this field. Even so, there were sculptors of

46   *Gaetano Previati (1852–1920) : The meadow. Galleria d'Arte Moderna, Florence.*

46 Gaetano Previati (1852–1920): *The meadow*. Galleria d'Arte Moderna, Florence.
Besides his impressionistic treatments of everyday subjects Previati painted imaginative canvases in which fact and fantasy are indistinguishably combined.

47 Gaetano Previati (1852–1920): *Our Lady of the Chrysanthemums*. Civica Galleria d'Arte Moderna, Milan.
Previati's madonnas are known for their ephemeral and insubstantial qualities and the suggestion they convey of great spirituality.

48 Giovanni Segantini (1858–99): *The two mothers* (detail). 1889. Civica Galleria d'Arte Moderna, Milan.
Segantini's use of chiaroscuro shows the influence of the Lombard school which he was to abandon in his later painting for a Neo-Impressionist style.

49 Giovanni Segantini (1858–99): *Love at the fountain of life. c* 1898. Civica Galleria d'Arte Moderna, Milan.
Segantini turned to a lighter palette and later still to allegorical subjects, which he painted with a wistful Symbolism.

50 Vittore Grubicy de Dragon (1851–1920): *Morning.* Civica Galleria d'Arte Moderna, Milan.
This comparatively minor work, rather too closely tied to academic habits, does nevertheless capture some of the qualities of morning sunlight.

51 Giuseppe Pellizza de Volpedo (1868–1907): *Children dancing in a ring.* Civica Galleria d'Arte Moderna, Milan.
The children playing in the lush grass are softly outlined in vibrant colours in a style that reveals its debt to Neo-Impressionism.

47

48   *Giovanni Segantini (1858–99) : The two mothers (detail). 1889.*
Civica Galleria d'Arte Moderna, Milan.

49   *Giovanni Segantini (1858–99) : Love at the fountain of life. c 1898.*
Civica Galleria d'Arte Moderna, Milan.

50   *Vittore Grubicy de Dragon (1851–1920)* :
Morning. Civica Galleria d'Arte Moderna, Milan.

51 *Giuseppe Pellizza da Volpedo (1868–1907) : Children dancing in a
ring. Civica Galleria d'Arte Moderna, Milan.*

great merit working at the time, the most considerable being Auguste Rodin and Medardo Rosso. These outstanding and original artists both owed something to Impressionism, even if it was only the new freedom that had been gained for modern art as a whole.

Rodin was educated in Paris at the peak of Impressionism. His sculpture expresses a restless vitality, an unceasing interest in experiment. His output was highly varied, ranging from the *bozzetto* (small sketch or model) to monumental figures. His basic style is evident even in his early work, and although he went through periods of revision and change the style of his mature years, with which he achieved his finest work, is remarkably consistent with the earlier period. Rodin knew how to use his material to suggest life, emotion and a three-dimensional kind of reality, to which he gave a bold and effective chiaroscuro finish. The very surface of his sculpture vibrates with an inner life that is quite independent of the overall composition.

Rodin was an accomplished draughtsman and he also drew some fine female nudes. His finest works were the *bozzetti* and single-subject sculptures. These range from the *Walking Man*, its rough finish so full of latent dynamism as it catches every change of light, to his stupendous *Monument* to Balzac, quite as brilliant as the genius it portrays. In his more complex monuments involving several figures Rodin seems to turn to the legacy of older sculptural traditions, from Late-Gothic Burgundian carving to the work of Michelangelo. And yet the heavy flowing garments and exaggerated gestures, especially of his later works, also have a certain grandiloquence that suggest a certain sympathy for the then current vein of Art

Nouveau. Indeed he seems at times to have succumbed to the influence of its somewhat artificial curvilinear forms, and what might be called its sensual restlessness. However, despite literary and symbolic tendencies that do not belong in the mainstream of twentieth century sculpture Rodin was greatly admired by successive generations and his work has provided an important and enduring source of inspiration. Among the lesser artists who followed his example Constantin-Emile Meunier is worthy of mention, most notably for his vigorously modelled male figures. One of his main interests, however, was in the social conditions of working men, and the political and humanitarian ideals that inspired his works tend also to lessen their artistic value.

Medardo Rosso was some years younger than Rodin; his early career involved him in the Scapigliatura movement in Lombardy, where he studied the style of Grandi and the 'unfinished' look he gave his sculpture. Later, when staying in Paris, he came into contact with the Impressionists and his ideas gained both in depth and intensity. Rosso's interest lay in conveying the fleeting, momentary quality of life, and thus his sculpture is marked by a return to great plasticity. His forms benefit greatly from conditions of light: in fact they are made to be seen from a single viewpoint, since only in a certain combination of light and shade do they convey the poetry and atmosphere intended by the sculptor. These are no longer self-sufficient, well-defined forms isolated in space, but open forms determined by space itself.

Rosso's favourite material was wax, because of its softness and malleability; his sculptures seem animated with secret vibrations that are not part of the

52   *Enrico Reycend (1855–1928) : A country cemetery. Galleria d'Arte Moderna, Turin.*

53 *Lorenzo Delleani (1840–1908) : The old flea-market, Turin. 1891.
Galleria d'Arte Moderna, Turin.*

52   Enrico Reycend (1855–1928): *A country cemetery*.
Galleria d'Arte Moderna, Turin.
This is a typical example of Reycend's painting, the rapid, intensive brushwork breaking up the composition in small zones of flattish colour.

53   Lorenzo Delleani (1840–1908): *The old flea-market, Turin*. 1891. Galleria d'Arte Moderna, Turin.
Lorenzo Delleani began to produce his rhythmic landscapes only from 1880.

54   Federico Zandomeneghi (1841–1917): *A last look*.
Galleria Internazionale d'Arte Moderna, Venice.
The influences of Renoir and Degas, who were great friends of the artist, are apparent in this canvas.

55   Giovanni Boldini (1842–1931): *The American woman*.
Civica Galleria d'Arte Moderna, Milan.
Boldini's gallery of society portraits, shows both freedom and spontaneity of a kind derived from the incisive brushwork of Toulouse-Lautrec.

56   Giuseppe de Nittis (1846–84): *The Place des Invalides*. Civica Galleria d'Arte Moderna, Milan.
Giuseppe de Nittis stayed in Paris and London, and caught the atmosphere of these two cities in the many views he painted, using a refined palette based on subtle tones of brown and grey.

57   Giuseppe de Nittis (1846–84): *Crossing the Apennines*. c 1867. Gallerie Nazionali di Capodimonte, Naples.
De Nittis, a Neopolitan, was an important regional figure in Italian art, who made great efforts to encourage other artists in Naples to experiment with new styles. In this work he shows a nice understanding of light and atmosphere.

54   *Federico Zandomeneghi (1841–1917) : A last look. Galleria
Internazionale d'Arte Moderna, Venice.*

55 *Giovanni Boldini (1842–1931) : The American woman. Civica Galleria d'Arte Moderna, Milan.*

56　*Giuseppe de Nittis (1846–84) : The Place des Invalides. Civica Galleria d'Arte Moderna, Milan.*

57 Giuseppe de Nittis (1846–84) : Crossing the Apennines. c 1867. Gallerie Nazionali di Capodimonte, Naples.

pictorial effect of the composition as a whole, but come from deep within the material; this itself seems to live and breathe.

Rosso was a sculptor of quite outstanding sensibility, able to convey the most fleeting impressions – the shy smile of a boy or the shadow of pain on a sick man's face. Misunderstood by his contemporaries Rosso was acclaimed by later generations, and his fame spread internationally.

At the same time another sculptor working in Naples became famous for his decorative and often highly expressive sculptures: these were simple, more realistic works and were often left as little more than *bozzetti*. His name was Vincenzo Gemito and his urchins and Neapolitan waifs have a certain charm, although like the painter Mancini he was sometimes content with superficial effects, and these have given his work a short-lived appeal, making him now appear rather parochial and dated.

Some of the general characteristics of Art Nouveau have already been mentioned in the context of late nineteenth century painting. However its influence was much greater in the field of architecture and the applied arts. This is because the movement was intimately connected with technical and industrial progress in the final decades of the nineteenth century.

Art Nouveau (or whatever it was called in the various countries where it flourished) had no obvious origins or originators who were chiefly responsible for it becoming known in Europe; in fact it was a very complex and almost self-propagating phenomenon that embraced various schools and independent centres of research and experimentation. In the end it was chiefly taken up by artists and, perhaps more important, architects from England, Scotland, Belgium, Germany, Austria and France. The basic theories of Art Nouveau are similar to those of the English Pre-Raphaelite movement, especially in the desire to give art a social significance by making it available to the masses and using it to communicate aesthetic values through a wide range of forms. The Art Nouveau architect did not limit himself to the design of houses alone, but also worked on their interior decoration; he provided sketches of the furniture and the practical domestic objects they were to contain. In the same way the graphic artist made designs for book covers, decorative panels, stained glass and so on. Art was used to spread its spiritual and cultural message to a wider public in a style that had as its keynote an orderly notion of elegance and harmony.

If the social theory was revolutionary, so too were the theories concerning the art itself. The prophets of the movement turned away from traditional formulas and found inspiration and new techniques in the developing world around them. Architects made use of new technical discoveries, building materials and methods of construction, and were prepared to adapt the conception and form a building to these new considerations. Decorators, cabinet-makers and ceramists made an enthusiastic attempt to produce to an industrial pattern, eagerly using all the working methods that industrial progress could put at their disposal. In every field there was a mature and intelligent acceptance of all that was implied by these innovations.

A pronounced taste for decoration was another characteristic feature of Art Nouveau. However, it

58 *Auguste Rodin (1840–1917) : The thinker. 1880. Musée Rodin, Paris.*

58 Auguste Rodin (1840–1917): *The thinker*. 1880. Musée Rodin, Paris.
The superb modelling of this famous figure allows great play with effects of light on the surface areas.

59 Auguste Rodin (1840–1917): *The kiss*. 1886. Musée Rodin, Paris.
Rodin shows a great concern for line and rhythm in this powerfully modelled group, in which the shadows as well as the figures themselves are arranged with powerful effect.

60 Auguste Rodin (1840–1917): *Flying figure*. 1890. Musée Rodin, Paris.
Rodin's vigorous lines draw the eye from one part of the body to the next; even the abruptly curtailed edges of his scheme exercise a powerful effect on the observer, turning him round and forcing him back into the intense heart of the composition.

61 Auguste Rodin (1840–1917): *The muse. c* 1896. Tate Gallery, London.
Made for the monument to Victor Hugo that was intended for the Panthéon, this figure was to represent the Muse of Meditation, lost in her dreams, gazing ecstatically at the poet.

62 Auguste Rodin (1840–1917): *Walking man*. 1905. Musée Rodin, Paris.
Rodin shows here the subtle, relaxed muscular action of the walker; although the movement is unhurried the entire body of the figure, the torso slightly tilted, is seen to be involved.

59 *Auguste Rodin (1840–1917) : The kiss. Musée Rodin, Paris.*

61   *Auguste Rodin (1840–1917) : The muse. c 1896. Tate Gallery, London.*

60   *Auguste Rodin (1840–1917) : Flying figure. 1890–1. Musée Rodin, Paris.*

107

was never used just for its own sake: in the new movement everything functional seems to be decorative and vice versa. Decoration included the most extraordinary variety of ornamental motifs; seaweed patterns, unusual forms of organic and inorganic life, abstract arabesques and geometric extravagances, always employed with great refinement, though also with a certain decadence. And, at least in the early days of Art Nouveau, there is a notable contrast between the ambition to create a practical and functional style, as expressed by leading figures in the movement, and the intellectual and sensual aspects of the same style; the latter often arose through the prevailing current of decadence and provided the most obvious visual characteristics of Art Nouveau. These conflicting tendencies in the new artistic vision were in fact highly typical of *fin-de-siècle* culture in Europe.

The first manifestations of Art Nouveau came in 1888, but its influence as a fashion and a way of life really spread through Europe only towards the end of the century. Shortly after 1880 the architect Mackmurdo published in London a book on English churches illustrated with flowing curvilinear drawings which had all the unmistakeable rhythms of the new style. It became known on the Continent and aroused great interest, especially in Belgium where two of the future leaders of Art Nouveau were studying – Henry van de Velde and Victor Horta.

Van de Velde infused his architectural designs with a rational and creative spirit. He built houses and designed furnishings according to strictly functional criteria; and while upholding the basic contemporary principle of a continuity of line and plane, he was to

62   *Auguste Rodin (1840–1917) : Walking man. 1905. Musée Rodin, Paris.*

63   *Medardo Rosso (1858–1928) : The concierge. 1883. Civica
Galleria d'Arte Moderna, Milan.*

64   *Medardo Rosso (1858–1928) : Flesh that belongs to others. 1883.*
Galleria Nazionale d'Arte Moderna, Rome.

63   Medardo Rosso (1858–1928): *The concierge.* 1883.
Civica Galleria d'Arte Moderna, Milan.
This is not a direct expression of reality so much as an
attempt to summon up the dream-like effect of a memory.

64   Medardo Rosso (1858–1928): *Flesh that belongs to
others.* 1883. Galleria Nazionale d'Arte Moderna, Rome.
The critic Ardengo Soffici has said of this work: 'The
sculptor shows all the misery of pleasure for sale in-
tensified and prolonged in the pathetic face of a tired girl'.

65   Medardo Rosso (1858–1928): *The bookmaker.* 1894.
Galleria Nazionale d'Arte Moderna, Rome.
The bookmaker, a transitory if stout figure complete with
top hat and binoculars and portrayed in the act of
staggering, almost threatens to dissolve back into the
material; in this way he is made to serve as his own
symbol.

66   Medardo Rosso (1858–1928): *Ecce puer.* 1906.
Civica Galleria d'Arte Moderna, Milan.
This was one of Rosso's last works and here he has used
a minimum of modelling to suggest the boy's face.

67   Vincenzo Gemito (1852–1929): *Head of a child.* 1872.
Galleria d'Arte Moderna, Turin.
Vincenzo Gemito used sensitive, delicate modelling to
make numerous sentimental heads of children, fishermen
and girls that nevertheless show his knowledge of contemporary French stylistic trends.

65   *Medardo Rosso (1858–1928) : The bookmaker. 1894.
Galleria Nazionale d'Arte Moderna, Rome.*

66 *Medardo Rosso (1858–1928) : Ecce puer. 1906. Civica Galleria d'Arte Moderna, Milan.*

67　*Vincenzo Gemito (1852–1929) : Head of a child. 1872.*
Galleria d'Arte Moderna, Turin.

achieve high levels of decorative elegance and simple, structural coherence – qualities that have become the hallmark of his buildings. Victor Horta had a freer and more fanciful style: the houses he designed in Brussels were also masterpieces of interior decoration, containing ultimately harmonious combinations of the most disparate decorative elements. His furniture is richly adorned with wrought iron and other curved metalwork and inlaid woods that never seem heavy or in any way superfluous.

Hendrik Petrus Berlage worked almost exclusively in Holland, where he began with a revolutionary adaptation of Romanesque forms, which became an original and truly modern architectural style based on solidly functional criteria. At the same time there was an enthusiastic reaction to the new movement in Austria and Germany, beginning with the Munich Secession in 1892 and then extending more widely via the periodicals *Pan* (1895), *Jugend* (1896) and *Ver Sacrum* (1898). The most active centres of Jugendstil, as it was known, were Berlin, Munich and Vienna. August Endell, the originator of the Elvira *atelier*, worked in Munich.

Endell claimed in his writings that every piece of furniture, like the exterior details of a house, should be in perfect harmony and make a homogeneous composition alike in character, form and effect. No element should attempt to be striking on its own; every detail should contribute to the overall style and correspond to the object next to it. Endell rigorously applied these principles in his best work, notably the Elvira *atelier* itself, and in smaller decorative items. In Austria Otto Wagner, Joseph Olbrich, Adolf Loos and Joseph Hoffman were enthused by similar ideas. There the

68   *Pierre Roche (1855–1922) : Loïe Fuller. c 1900.*
Musée des Arts Décoratifs, Paris.

68   Pierre Roche (1855–1922): *Lôie Fuller. c* 1900. Musée des Arts Décoratifs, Paris.
Every night in a Paris club Loïe Fuller performed her dance with swirling veils under multicoloured lights to enthusiastic audiences that included many famous artists. In this work Roche has created a symbolic image by seeming to fuse the veils with the body beneath.

69   Eugène Grasset (1841–1917): *Spring* (stained glass). 1884. Musée des Arts Décoratifs, Paris.
Eugène Grasset was an architect and was interested in all forms of applied art; he showed a preference for using decorations inspired by natural forms.

70   Émile Gallé (1846–1904): Vase decorated with a dragonfly motif. 1887. Musée des Arts Décoratifs, Paris. The dragonfly motif appears often in Gallé's work; he was the leading artist of the Ecole de Nancy, and his work inspired the American, Louis Comfort Tiffany.

71   Auguste (1853–1909) and Antonin (1864–1930) Daum: Lamp and vase. Private Collection, Milan.
The sons of Jean Daum, Auguste and Antonin carried on their father's work and their style became increasingly similar to the fluid lines and imitation of natural forms that characterize the work of Émile Gallé.

69   *Eugène Grasset (1841–1917)* : *Spring (stained glass)*. *1884. Musée des Arts Décoratifs, Paris.*

70 *Émile Gallé (1846–1904) : Vase decorated with a dragonfly motif. 1887. Musée des Arts Décoratifs, Paris.*

71   *Auguste (1853–1909) and Antonin (1864–1930) Daum : Lamp and vase.*
Private Collection, Milan.

sinuous decorative line typical of Olbrich alternates with severely plain buildings, designed according to the Austrian preference for sobriety.

At the same time one of the most outstanding talents of European architecture was at work in Glasgow – Charles Rennie Mackintosh. His buildings are a combination of the functional and the imaginative, while his most modern and ingenious structures demonstrate a perfect harmony of rectilinear forms and curvilinear surfaces employing decorations of plant and marine motifs. The overall effect is musical and is enhanced by the lightness of the colours, which blend perfectly with the other elements of his style. Mackintosh's best known architectural work is his Glasgow School of Art; in interior design he produced, among other schemes, furniture and complete settings for four Glasgow tea rooms for a Miss Kate Cranston that were influential in spreading the new style.

Art Nouveau reached France later than many other parts of Europe; however, the movement there was more widespread and long-lived. In architecture the leading exponent was Guimard, best known today for his Paris *métro* entrances. Perret was a contemporary but his taste for decoration was always modified by an instinctive classicism. There was also Garnier, whose use of new techniques such as re-inforced concrete opened the way for modern architecture. Italy's contribution to the architecture of Art Nouveau was relatively unimportant. In Lombardy the work of Sommaruga is worthy of mention; the ornamental plant motifs that adorn the exteriors of his buildings offer some of the best examples of the Stile of the Floreale, which Sommaruga introduced to Italy.

72 *Henry van de Velde (1863–1948) : The architect's house at Uccle, Brussels. 1896.*

72 Henry van de Velde (1863–1948): The architect's house at Uccle, Brussels. 1896.

Van de Velde, with no previous experience, committed all his architectural theories to the test by designing and building his own house.

73 Victor Horta (1861–1947): Maison Solvay, Brussels. 1895.

This is one of the finest of Horta's designs: the rhythmic complexity of its façade is broken up by transept-like divisions and metal columns; the house still contains its original furniture designed by the architect.

74 Hendrik Petrus Berlage (1856–1934): The Union of Diamond Workers' Building, Amsterdam. 1899–1900.

Although Berlage was inspired by medieval architecture he also tried to design buildings based on utilitarian considerations which would be relevant to contemporary life.

75 Joseph Hoffman (1870–1956): Palais Stoclet, Brussels. 1905–14.

The clean lines of this industrialist's house are interrupted only by the window apertures; the walls are clad in sheets of white Norwegian marble and four marble athletes adorn the tower.

76 Otto Wagner (1841–1918): The Majolika Haus, Vienna.

This house, with its highly original façade of ceramic floral decoration, was designed in 1898.

73   *Victor Horta (1861–1947) : Maison Solvay ; Brussels. 1895.*

74 *Hendrik Petrus Berlage (1856–1934) : The Union of Diamond Workers' Building, Amsterdam. 1899–1900.*

75 *Joseph Hoffmann (1870–1956) : Palais Stoclet, Brussels.
1905–1914.*

Antoni Gaudi deserves a special place in the story of Art Nouveau. He was the leading figure of a group of artists in Barcelona and was responsible for the modernization of Spanish culture that inspired Picasso as a young artist. Gaudi participated fully in the spirit of Art Nouveau, and his work is an expression of its refined and fanciful exuberance and decorative lyricism. And yet he was basically quite independent of the experiments being carried out in the other great European centres; he worked only in Barcelona and was not affected by other examples of Art Nouveau architecture in France, Scotland, Belgium and Germany – in fact he himself was hardly known outside Spain. Thus without any direct influence from elsewhere he evolved an original style that is typical of the creative vigour and strength inherent in all great Spanish architecture.

After an initial period of interest in the Late-Gothic style his own originality revealed itself in buildings such as the House and Park designed for Count Güell, and the unfinished façade of the Church of the Sagrada Familia. In these buildings the stone seems to be moulded like molten lava into fantastic shapes; every element is incorporated in an overall scheme of unbridled decorative exuberance; the sinuous façades are adorned with wrought iron balconies; the perforated spires of the Sagrada Familia suggest complex vegetable growth. Gaudi loved to combine different materials, using coloured ceramics, rough stones and especially metalwork, which he applied in a highly original way, making them blend, too, with the natural surroundings.

The social function of art, which was greatly debated at the turn of the century, favoured a widespread

76 *Otto Wagner (1841–1918) : The Majolika Haus, Vienna.*

77 *Charles Rennie Mackintosh (1868–1928) : Library wing, Glasgow School of Art. 1907–9.*

78 *Hector Guimard (1867–1942) : Entrance to a Paris métro station.*
1898–1901.

77 Charles Rennie Mackintosh (1868–1928): Library Wing, Glasgow School of Art. 1907–9.
The massive School of Art, Mackintosh's most celebrated work, was built in 1898–9 and enlarged ten years later with a library wing and other extensions.

78 Hector Guimard (1867–1942): Entrance to a Paris métro station. 1898–1901.
Guimard is especially famous for his entrances to Paris métro stations made in delicate and flexible metal that so fully express the linear, ornamental spirit of Art Nouveau.

79 Antoni Gaudi (1852–1926): Entrance to the Parco Güell, Barcelona (detail). 1900–14.
Gaudi was commissioned by the industrialist Güell to design a park similar in plan to the English garden-city. The result was a highly original scheme both in terms of layout and architecture, the houses following an 'organic' plan featuring cones and sweeping parabolas decorated with bright mosaics.

80 Antoni Gaudi (1852–1926): The Façade of the Nativity, Church of the Sagrada Familia, Barcelona. 1909–26.
Although the basic design of this unfinished church was obviously Neo-Gothic Gaudi's quite unconventional brilliance, which is evident in all his most daring constructions, has made it a dazzling and totally original building.

79 Antoni Gaudi (1852–1926) : Entrance to the Parco Güell, Barcelona (detail). 1900–14.

development of many forms of decorative art and a gradual transformation in all fields from craftsmanship to a more industrialized scheme of production, helped by technical progress. In France the Ecole Céramique de Nancy was changed in 1901 to become the Alliance Provinciale des Industries d'Art. The founder of the school, Emile Gallé, was originally a glassmaker who later experimented in ceramics and furnishings and together with the architect Guimard, the decorator Plumet and the cabinet-maker Majorelle had an important influence on the development of Art Nouveau in France. He was responsible for the widespread popularity of floral-style ceramics and the development of their sinuous curvilinear decorations, their tendrils and interwoven, complex designs clothed in symbolical significance; he also worked with furniture, using inlaid woods, mother-of-pearl incrustations and metalwork ornaments.

Metal, and more especially iron, was widely used in the applied arts during this period. It decorated furniture, railings and smaller objects such as lamps, vases, candle-holders and other ornamental pieces that may be seen as sculptures in their own right. With their thin stems and delicate supports they open into drooping corollas, designed in conformity with that febrile obsession with the decorative line that came to pervade all art forms in those years. The same can be said of glass objects, which appear even more fragile because of their delicate material.

Nearly all of Europe was involved in this new artistic fashion. In Austria the technique of bending wood with steam, developed in the Vienna factory of Thonnet, facilitated the mass-production of furniture, especially of stylized and sinuous chairs decorated

80 *Antoni Gaudi (1852–1926) : Façade of the Nativity,*
Church of the Sagrada Familia, Barcelona. 1909–26.

with characteristic curvilinear motifs on the backs, arms and legs. At the beginning of the twentieth century Philip Rosenthal in Germany discovered how to mass-produce high-quality floral-style ceramics. In Belgium and in Germany van de Velde popularized a taste for stylized furniture that was both refined and severe, the emphasis being on functional qualities rather than decorative elegance. In England the nineteenth century had seen the development of the Arts and Crafts movement through the activities of William Morris. Closely linked with the Pre-Raphaelites' theories it had an important influence on the development of Art Nouveau in that it was based on the idea of functional art, where form and use are interdependent. From these beginnings developed the elaborate and audaciously modern style initiated by the work of Mackintosh.

Although Art Nouveau suffers at times from a recurring vein of artificiality and decadence, and from the occasional monotony of its obsessional curvilinear motifs, it was still an extraordinarily important movement, above all for shaping modern attitude, to art and its relationships with society, which it defined and fostered in all fields.

In this climate of crisis and experiment some of the most important figures of twentieth century art were influenced by the conflicting trends at work in their youth, before they came to develop their own styles.

In 1900 Pablo Picasso came to Paris. Born in Malaga in 1881, he spent his adolescence first in Corunna and then mainly in Barcelona. As a child Picasso had shown a talent for drawing and painting and later in Barcelona he worked intensively on a series of canvases; these largely followed traditional Spanish work

81   *J. Juriaen Kok and J. Schelling : Bottle-vase.*
Österreichisches Museum für Angewandte Kunst, Vienna.

137

81   J. Juriaen Kok and J. Schelling: Bottle-vase. Österreichisches Museum für Angewandte Kunst, Vienna.
This bottle-vase shape was designed by Kok for the
Rosenburg company; the refined plant-form decoration
that enhances and accentuates the flowing shape is the
work of his collaborator, Schelling.

82   Franz Hoosemans: Candelabra in silver and ivory.
Maison Solvay, Brussels.
The ivory figure of the woman, with her flowing seaweed
hair, is delicately contrasted with the floral motif of the
silver candle-holders.

83   Alexandre Charpentier (1856–1909): Revolving Lectern. 1901. Musée des Arts Décoratifs, Paris.
This carved lectern has a remarkably sensual stem and is
probably the best work of Charpentier, a French
furniture-maker who was at one time active in Brussels.

84   Richard Riemerschmid (1868–1957): Chair. Stadtmuseum, Munich.
Riemerschmid was an architect, decorator and artist who
designed many chairs and seats in a variety of forms, all
characterized by their functional elegance.

83   *Alexandre Charpentier (1856–1909) : Revolving
lectern. 1901. Musée des Arts Décoratifs, Paris.*

84   *Richard Riemerschmid (1868–1957) : Chair.*
Stadtmuseum, Munich.

but at the same time he was inspired by realism and its applications to social criticism. His early works exhibited in Paris have the same characteristics; his subjects are taken from the simple lives of poor folk and records their dramas and sorrows. The style is harsh and vigorous with a note of bitterness, and seems somehow a logical synthesis of the passionate violence of Spanish painting and the critical, incisive, graphic excellence of Toulouse-Lautrec. For he was Picasso's master in this first period in France, and the young Spaniard greatly admired his realistic scenes of the equivocal, restless life of Montmartre and its sad world of corruption recorded by Lautrec in the *boîtes de nuit*.

However, Picasso's style soon evolved along different lines and he entered what is known as his Blue Period (1901–4). Here Lautrec's influence is still apparent but Picasso's own style seems more resolutely original in its treatment of the themes of popular humanitarianism already mentioned in the context of other artists of the time. His figures, whether single or in groups, are almost exclusively working-class: workmen, children, beggars – they are drawn with a bold outline that enhances their thin, emaciated forms. In these canvases Picasso manages to convey all the intensity of human suffering, silent loneliness and the blackest despair with a quite exemplary economy of expression. Blue, the symbol of night and sorrow, is the dominant colour of this work and already the twenty-year-old artist shows a happy fusion of French stylistic trends and the desolate world of grief familiar to the Spanish mind. It is already apparent that this young man was destined to become a leading figure in twentieth century art.

85   *René-Jules Lalique (1860–1945) : Diadem with siren. Musée des Arts Décoratifs, Paris.*

85   René-Jules Lalique (1860–1945): *Diadem with siren.*
Musée des Arts Décoratifs, Paris.
René-Jules Lalique created many decorative glass objects,
but he was best known for his imaginative jewellery
formed of intricate designs and opulent flowing shapes.

86   Emile-Antoine Bourdelle (1861–1929): *Hercules the
Archer.* 1909. Metropolitan Museum of Art, New York;
gift of Mr and Mrs Stephen C. Millet, 1924.
Bourdelle returned many times to the theme of this his
finest work; it is a brilliant expression of strength at the
moment of its transformation into action.

87   Aristide Maillol (1861–1944): *Portrait of Renoir.*
1907. Niedersächsisches Landesmuseum, Hanover.
Maillol, influenced by Gauguin and the Nabis, with whom
he exhibited until 1903, only took up sculpture at around
the turn of the century; he concentrated on the female
nude, but this portrait is typical of his sensibility and
restraint.

88   Aristide Maillol (1861–1944): *Night.* 1902. Kunstmuseum, Winterthur.
Maillol's female nudes are famous; this early example is
somewhat simplified and has a solid, strangely (for
Maillol) monumental character.

86   *Emile-Antoine Bourdelle (1861–1929) : Hercules the Archer. 1909.*
Metropolitan Museum of Art, New York.

87   *Aristide Maillol (1861–1944) : Portrait of Renoir. 1907.*
Niedersächsisches Landesmuseum, Hanover.

88   *Aristide Maillol (1861–1944) : Night. 1902. Kunstmuseum, Winterthur.*

Georges Rouault was ten years older than Picasso but he painted his first 'social' works at about the same time; they show with dramatic vividness a world of clowns, working people and prostitutes. He had previously frequented the *atelier* of Gustave Moreau and had painted canvases of biblical scenes characterized by intense zones of colour enclosed within heavy black outlines (a technique he had learnt when apprenticed to a stained-glass designer). At Moreau's in the last decades of the nineteenth century were also Henri Matisse, Albert Marquet and others of the future Fauve movement. It is significant of the period that Matisse, the master of the Fauvist style, was then experimenting freely with the numerous possibilities put forward by various great masters of the nineteenth century and that, in consequence, his paintings show the obvious influences of the Impressionists, the Post-Impressionists and the Nabis, as well as a calligraphic element that is more typical of Art Nouveau.

89   *Pablo Picasso (1881– 1973) : The blind man's meal.* **1903**. *Metropolitan Museum of Art, New York.*

91   *Pablo Picasso (1881– 1973) : La Vie.* **1903.** *Cleveland Museum of Art, Cleveland, Ohio.*

90   *Pablo Picasso (1881–1973) : The flower seller.* **1901.** *Art Gallery and Museum, Glasgow.*

89   Pablo Picasso (born 1881): *The blind man's meal.* 1903. Metropolitan Museum of Art, New York.
This humble figure, mute and suffering, is typical of Picasso's Blue Period when he showed great concern for social problems, involving his quest for revelations concerning man's innermost nature.

90   Pablo Picasso (born 1881): *The flower seller.* 1901. Art Gallery and Museum, Glasgow.
This work arose from Picasso's second stay in Paris: the young Spanish artist was variously influenced by the style and subject-matter of the Impressionists and Divisionists, by Toulouse-Lautrec, van Gogh, Gauguin and the Nabis.

91   Pablo Picasso (born 1881): *La Vie.* 1903. Cleveland Museum of Art, Cleveland, Ohio.
Picasso's work at this time shows him moving away from contemporary currents towards a statuesque manner of his own that was further unified by a mood of melancholy and the use of cold blue tones.

92   Georges Rouault (1871–1958): *Prostitute at her Mirror.* 1906. Musée National d'Art Moderne, Paris.
Rouault's dramatic compositions marked by an emotional use of colour and heavy outlines established him after the turn of the century as the leading French Expressionist painter.

92   *Georges Rouault (1871–1958) : Prostitute at her mirror. 1906. Musée National d'Art Moderne, Paris.*

BIBLIOGRAPHY

M. BATTERSBY, Art Nouveau, London & New York 1969

O. BENESCH, Edvard Munch, London 1960

R. COGNIAT, Bonnard, New York 1968

J. P. HODIN, Edvard Munch, New York 1970

I. JIANOU, Rodin, New York

R. PANE, Antoni Gaudi, Milan 1964

J. PORUCHO, Gaudi : An Architecture of Anticipation, New York 1968

B. READE, Art Nouveau & Alphonse Mucha, London and New York 1968

A. C. RITCHIE, Vuillard, New York

A. RODIN, Ed. S. STORY, Rodin : Sculptures, New York 1964

R. SCHMUTZLER, Art Nouveau, New York 1964

LIST OF ILLUSTRATIONS

157